Biblioteens

Bibliotoons

A Mischievous Meander Through the Stacks & Beyond

by
Gary Handman
with a Foreword
by Art Plotnik

McFarland & Company, Inc., Publishers
Jefferson, North Carolina & London

British Library Cataloguing-in-Publication data are available

Library of Congress Cataloguing-in-Publication Data

Handman, Gary, 1950—
    Bibliotoons : a mischievous meander through the stacks and beyond.

    Includes bibliographical references.
    1. Libraries-- Caricatures and cartoons.
2. Library science--Caricatures and cartoons.
3. Information science--Caricatures and cartoons. I. Title.
    Z682.5.H35 1990   020'.207   89-13620
    ISBN 0-89950-481-7 (55# alk. paper) ∞

Printed in the United States of America

McFarland & Company, Inc., Publishers
Box 611, Jefferson, North Carolina
28640

830259

FOR
Pammy & Becky
with much love!

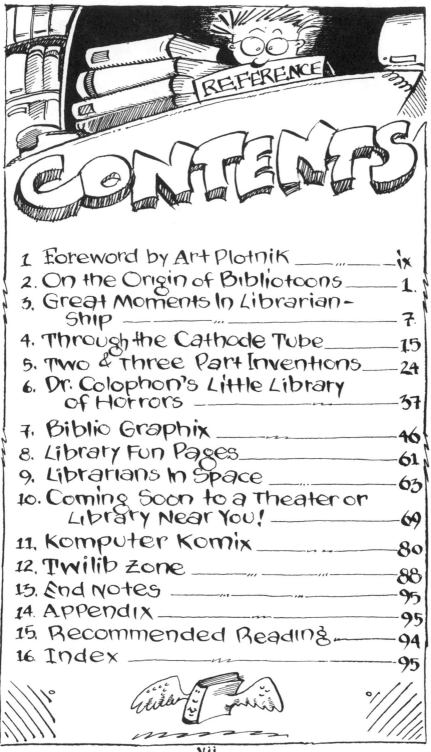

CONTENTS

Foreword

by Art Plotnik

BEFORE GARY HANDMAN SMASHED the biblio-barrier, only one comic library drawing had ever squeezed a laugh out of this editorial stone. The drawing showed a face-down murder victim skewered by a catalog rod—the kind that used to hold 3 × 5 cards in the old catalog trays.

The new use was amusing; but the artist, a librarian, lacked one of two essential attributes for the bibliographic cartooning game. Although he had deep library savvy, which is one essential, he cartooned about as well as the artists who do cocktail napkins.

Professional-level cartooning skill, plus an inside understanding of what's funny to librarians: We are talking about the rarest combination since Mantle and Maris. Because Gary Handman is one of the solar system's few organisms with both attributes, his works are collector's items. They deserve their enshrinement in this special collection.

Why is inside savvy so important in library humor? Because most "outsider" library gags play on the worst stereotypes of shushing librarians or the silliest notions of what goes on in the stacks. Every other day, it seems, *American Libraries* receives a drawing of Rip Van Winkle returning his overdue books; or of some masked jerk loitering in the "Mysteries" section; or of a schlemiel climbing a pile of books to the section marked "Mountain Climbing." Did any library ever *have* a section marked Mountain Climbing?

Handman, who earned his library degree in 1976 from the University of California–Berkeley, finds more comedy in

MARC fields and serials control than in schlemiels climbing the stacks. He is an accomplished library professional, who, during work hours, applies himself with Clark Kent intensity.

He began as a special librarian for the Bechtel Corporation, where, in the seventies, he could run circles around Bechtel colleagues George Shultz and Caspar Weinberger when it came to loading microfilm readers. At Berkeley, he was Numero Two in the Acquisitions Department before his ascension to head, Media Resources Center. As a librarian he has done it all: tech services, reference, administration, and schmoozing at high-level professional meetings. Thus Handman has encountered all the library follies, apprehensions, frustrations, doubletalk, and fatuous nonsense that any cartoonist would ever need to blow this profession into comic Kingdom Come—provided the cartooning ability was there.

"I guess I always had it," says Handman, who received no formal training in art. But in sixth grade, he did receive a threat from a bully who liked his doodlings: "You keep doin' 'em or else!" the bully told him. Handman kept doin' 'em.

In the early eighties, Handman's wife Pam—also a librarian—got fed up seeing his doodlings appear on any available surface. She bought him a drafting table, and from that point Handman got serious about humor.

His first drawings appeared in the Bay Area Special Libraries Association *Bulletin*, then went national in *Special Libraries*. But it was *American Libraries* that gave him the full, four-color exposure that has made him the most sought-after illustrator in the library/information field. When a sodden piece of library literature has to somehow sing its way into the hearts of readers, only a Handman *Bibliotoon* will help.

Whatever the cartooning task, Handman's observant, understated, fluid touch works magic. Sketching an American Library Association conference for *American Libraries*, he captured in just four or five strokes a petite speaker boring the doubleknits off a vast conference crowd. His style is immediately recognizable: those straight-up-and-down, spike-haired victims of library life, those harried librarians and bewildered patrons as innocent as little Fisher-Price people.

The Handmans live in Berkeley with their baby daughter Rebecca and their dog Nick — a wire-haired fox terrier who figures in many drawings and who runs their lives.

Handman says that as an undergraduate he studied anthropology and film — "in other words, nonreality." That and the library degree seem to have been good preparation for his unique views of Libraryland — and the many nonrealities that endear it to us.

September 1989

(Art Plotnik was the editor of American Libraries *from 1975 to 1989, and became associate publisher of the American Libraries Association in 1989.)*

xi

"...A circulating library in a town is as an evergreen tree of diabolical knowledge! It blossoms throughout the year! And depend on it ... that they who are so fond of handling the leaves will long for the fruit at last.

— Richard Sheridan
"The Rivals" (Act I, Sc. 2)

ON THE ORIGIN OF BIBLIOTOONS

REFERENCE

Two things I've learned about this library humor business: easy or inexhaustible it ain't!! I mean a guy like charles schulz is blessed with what is an apparently bottomless gold mine of strip material — maybe he has tapped some Jungian vein in the universal psyche with those light bulb-headed kids of his, who knows? What I do know is that Mr. S can have sadistic little Lucy pull the ball out from under poor nebbishy charlie Brown from now until the polar ice caps melt, and the public (not to mention the licensing Lords of Commerce) will continue to eat it up. Now, compare my lonely plight. Somehow, a career based on MARC delimiter gags doesn't seem to be on exactly the same kind of funnies fast track. And as far as large junk food companies knocking eagerly on my door for the rights to put Mr. Authority Control on their shrink-wrap... I'm not quitting my day job just yet.

But still... dealing with the public as much as we do (and most certainly with the electronic gizmos which have become our stock in trade) is bound to provide a fair amount of grist for the old proverbial humor mill. There's also something inherently funny (in my book, at least)

Take my successive entry cataloging.... PLEASE!!

about the wildly specialized and arcane tools and terms in any profesbox. And Lord knows sion's tool-librarianship has enough acronyms, initialisms, buzzwords, and cabal-istic professional rites to sink at least two ships (bound for the IFLA conference in Borneo, perhaps?),

riends and colleagues who know about my doodling have frequently asked me if I get the ideas for this stuff during work hours - at the reference desk, for example. The notion of acting as a quill- wielding secret recorder of professional foibles and fantasies sounds terribly romantic, and I'd love to say that's what I do (sort of Thomas Nast meets Daumier meets Garry Trudeau). Unfortunately, after a few hours of pawing thru the Europa Yearbook for the GNP of Latvia, or attempting to explain for the twentieth time in a shift that the online catalog is, in fact, neither divine nor mephistophelian, my humor quotient is, I admit, often shot. More often, the gags come to mind long after I've left the front lines, at home, say, with a few glasses o' vino to prime the free association pump. Sometimes, my subconscious obliges by doing the pratfalling for me at 2AM, tossing out horrible puns and situations even more surreal than those encountered during the day shift.

This is not to say that the trenches don't yield their share of goofy raw material. Like the hapless freshman attempting to dig into reading for his midterm. After a half hour of sparring with the OPAC, he came crawling to the desk with that familiar look of panic and cosmic confusion, begging for the works of "Russo and

Gerta" ("The machine says you don't have any-
thing!"). After he stopped hyperventilating,
we played the old 20 questions and determined
that just maybe what the instructor had in mind

were not the memoirs of some Italian/Swedish
vaudeville team, but instead, the writings of
Mssr. Rousseau and Herr Goethe.

This kind of amusing auditory scramble
occurs on both sides of the desk. Witness
the harried colleague who persisted in sending
an increasingly perplexed patron back to reference works on inventions and inventors in
response to what was interpreted as a request
for "background on rubber bands." When the
exasperated patron finally insisted that these
sources contained not even a small footnote on
the topic, they went back to the bibliographic
drawing board, finally determining that what
was really being asked for was a history of the
Robber Barons (so much for The Way Things
Work!!)

Vanderbilt's
the name!!
Rubber bands
are the game!

Catalogs (and cata-
logers) frequently
provide the kinds of
bibliographic pies-in-the-
face that are the stuff
great gags are made of. Take
for example the handiwork of
a perverse, dyslexic, or sleepy
cataloger discovered in the course
of a routine (!!!) keyword
search for material on ursine
mating habits. Perhaps the
aforementioned cataloger had
taken to heart projected plans
to merge biology and agriculture collections.
Maybe he or she was a closet biotechnology
fan with clones on the brain. Or perhaps it
was someone getting even with a junior high
typing teacher ("watch those "p's" and "b's,"
people!") In any case, the search

turned up several <u>very</u> interesting items on growing and harvesting Bartlett Bears. There's also the time it was discovered that some tech services rogue had been surreptitiously entering, let us say, very "colorful" limericks into the online system: "There was a young stud from Lc..." Ahem! Try finding subfields for those!!!

Bartlett's Familiar Bears

Undoubtedly my favorite potential cartoon situation, however, popped up a few months ago on the desk of a colleague in my library. Now, the fellow in question is one of the finest reference librarians I know — something of a bibliographic éminence grise around our place. He's the kind of librarian who never ceases to wow you with useful and amazing facts pulled like rabbits from a seemingly magical professional hat: <u>Tabor's Medical Dictionary</u> has a table of phobias at back; <u>Sludge Magazine</u> is indexed in <u>Silt & Effluence Abstracts</u>, and so on. The neatly typed inquiry which mysteriously landed on his desk was from a local junior high student, and with it, my reference pundit friend may have finally met his match. It read very simply and sweetly: "Dear librarian please send me all the information you have on the future."

YOGI Datananda knows ALL

I could go on, I suppose, about the weird things people do when they attempt to talk to machines. One wonderfully cracked example involved a flamboyantly off-kilter patron encountered during an otherwise unmemorable Sunday nite shift.

14.

Through the Cathode Tube

Through the Cathode Tube

OR
Alice's Adventures in Infoland
(with profound apologies to the Rev. Dodgson)

One thing was for certain, that the spell-checker had had nothing to do with it — it was the thesaurus' fault entirely. Alice had been gazing dreamily at the word processor for hours. "Goodness!" she finally cried to no one in particular. "At this rate, I'll never get the annual report done! The circ and reference stats are only half done, and I haven't even begun the spreadsheet for staff expenditures yet!!" Alice looked at the screen again and suddenly shook her head angrily. "And to make matters worse," she muttered, "I've used the terms 'labor-intensive' and 'cost-effective' six times each on the first page! This will never, never do!" As she leaned forward to click her mouse, a most curious thing happened...

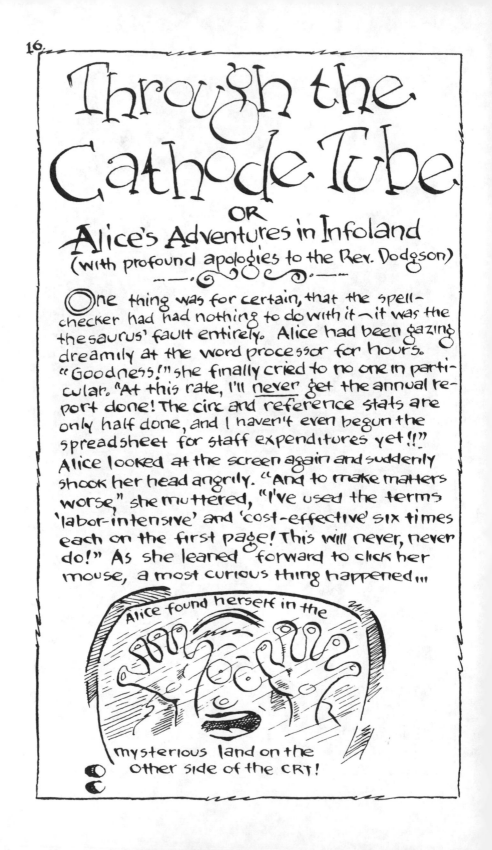

Alice found herself in the mysterious land on the other side of the CRT!

The Vendor & the Technophile

The monitor was glowing brite,
 All green and glassed
  and smug.
Its phosphore eye was
 fixed and stern
Within its cathode mug
And this was odd, because
 no one had yet pushed
 in the plug.

The discs were singing in their drives,
 The heads skipped
  with delight
The EGA adapter drew
 Some very graphic sights
And hungry random
 memory cried out for
 bit and byte.

The vendor and the technophile
 Were walking close at hand
They wished most earnestly to have
 More money to expand.
"If budgets were accordions,
 we'd play to beat the band!"

"If ten percent of all book dough
 were used to buy new toys,
Do you suppose," the Techy asked,
 "we'd hear opposing noise?"
"Most probably!" the vendor moaned,
 Losing all his poise.

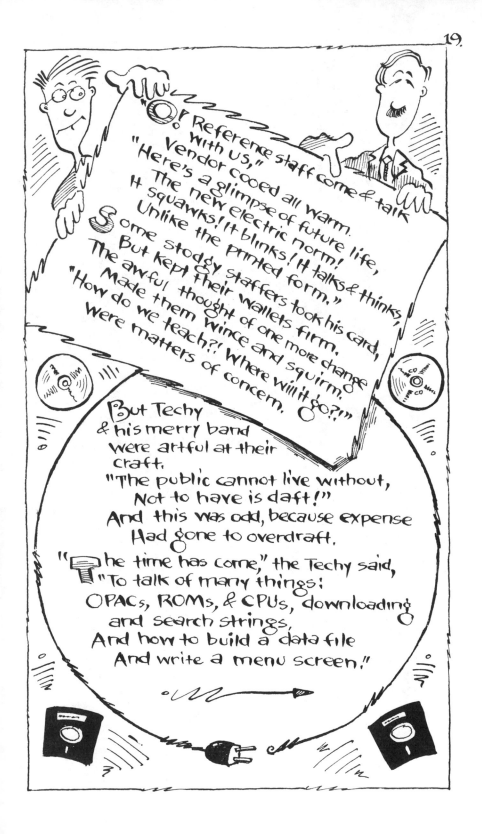

"O! Reference staff come & talk
with us," Vendor cooed all warm.
"Here's a glimpse of future life,
The new electric norm!"

Unlike the printed form,
It squawks! It blinks! It talks & thinks,
Some stodgy staffers took his card,
But kept their wallets firm.

The awful thought of one more change
Made them wince and squirm.
"How do we teach?! Where will it go?!"
Were matters of concern.

But Techy
& his merry band
were artful at their
craft.
"The public cannot live without,
Not to have is daft!"
And this was odd, because expense
Had gone to overdraft.

"The time has come," the Techy said,
"To talk of many things:
OPACs, ROMs, & CPUs, downloading
and search strings,
And how to build a data file
And write a menu screen."

So sweet they crooned, such tales they told,
That Peter gave to Paul
Plugs grew like wild geraniums
On every desk and wall,
And LANS crept like electric asps
'Neath floor, on roof, et al.

"Now, aren't you glad," the Vendor crowed,
"You've gone the 'lectric route?
Your access has increased tenfold,
Just as I did tout!!
The only things you have to fear—
Obsolescence & blackouts"

He bid the Tech a fond 'adieu!
Good-bye and luck, old sport!
We're with you in this all the way
Just call product support,"
And with these words he disappeared
With wicked vendor snort.

Once Alice fell back to earth she found herself on a path lined with large oak drawers. In the distance, a regiment of soldiers came marching in strict alphabetical order. They were followed by their senile monarch, the Queen of cards,

— Nothing before something!
Nothing before something!!

Read

Are you converted, my Dear?

The Queen and her army came to a sudden stop in front of Alice — so sudden that many cards in the army tumbled over one another. The Samuel Clemens fell into Mark Twain's position, and Thomas Stearns Eliot became plain old T. S. "Now look what you've done!" said the Queen.

"You have made me a very cross reference! Off with her head!!" "But your 3½ by 5ness...," Alice began to protest. "Don't be impertinent," said the Queen. "Here's a riddle: 'how many catalogers does it take to plug in a computer?'" When Alice gave up, the Queen shouted: "Two!! One to hold the plug and one to look up how L.C. does it. Here's another," said the Queen: "Where's the restroom?" Alice was about to confess her ignorance when a large white rabbit came bounding by. "What excellent signage!" cried Alice, clapping her hands. "I wonder if it was done on a Mac!" The Queen, however, was by now interested in other things. She motioned to Alice to sit beside her.

"Now hush, child!"
said the Queen. "It's
story hour!" And
this is the tale
she told...

The Datatalky

Twas modem and the PC clones
  Did boot and RAM cache kilobytes.
All memorish were the silicones,
  The pixels were a sight.

Beware the Datatalk, my friend,
  The link that fails, the garbled cite.
Beware false drops and be on guard
  For jammy printer blight!

They took their good password in hand
  Long time the nested search they sought
So logged they on with strategy planned,
  And non-prime time they bought.

And as they waited for connect
  The Datatalk with online guile
O'er telephone line slid circumspect
  And snortled "What's the file?"

And Or! And Not! Expand! Select!
  With Boolean blade all honed and hot
They searched free-text, descriptor strings,
  And then combined the lot

"And hast thou search results, good friend?
  Come give to me the printed form!
Calloo, Callee! That's quite a fee!"
  He grumbled in rebuff

Twas modem, and the pc clones...

The Queen finished her story abruptly and fixed Alice with a most impolite stare. "How are an escape artist and a serial alike?" the Queen asked suddenly. But before Alice could offer her answer, the Queen blurted out: "Because both enjoy being bound periodically!" And with this, she turned an alarming shade of blue. "Your Majesty is not well!" cried Alice. "Nonsense!!!!" sniffed the Queen. "It is simply because I am frozen! The Rector of Retrospection will be at the tea-party—he will convert me; that always seems to work wonders!"

Alice followed the Queen to a great hall, in which a most peculiar party was in progress,

After a short time in the company of this strange lot, Alice's head began to ache, and her eyes grew heavy. Then she awoke. But the annual report was still unfinished,

TWO AND THREE PART INVENTIONS FOR LIBRARIES

⊕ PAT. PEND.

Great "Reference" Escapes

Crusty but influential academic type Ⓐ approaches desk with weighty ontological question. Librarian Ⓑ forgets what ontological means and blushes furiously. Addled fireman Ⓒ thinks something's burning, cranks victrola instead of fire pump. Tango record causes dancing bear Ⓓ to shimmy. Vibration knocks tome into basket Ⓔ, pulling rope, which switches on Masterpiece Theatre Ⓕ. Patron's attention is diverted to Alistair Cooke, thus allowing librarian to sneak into stacks to consult O.E.D.

Device for Cutting Serial Expenditures

Collection development librarian reviews latest serial inflation figures and gets hot under collar①. Heat sets off smoke alarm②, which activates fire extinguisher③. Water from extinguisher grows rubber plant④. Myopic gardener⑤ moves in to clip vegetation, prunes serial list instead.

Device for Low-Budget Rural I.L.L.

SOOEY! SOOEY!! HF75.5.A62

Extra large agenda

ZZZZZ

AGENDA

Portable microfilm reader

Mechanisms for using time productively during boring committee meetings

TOYS
CONTINUED
I WANT NOW!
Gimme answer!
NOW!
Where the Wild Patrons Are
ALSO
MR AUTHORITY CONTROL
Hand puppet
A
B
DATABASE SEARCHING
THESAURUS
THE SEARCHER IS IN
FEES
$
Page from 1st folio Dr. Seuss
JUNIOR CONSERVATOR SET
PH
MR DEACIDIFICATION KIT

Multimedia Mechanism
For Curing Insomnia

Insomniac collapses into comfy chair, activating spring mechanisms, which provide access to: (A) AACR II (B) Audiocassette of library school lecture entitled "The Joys of Analytics" (C) Video of James Billington leading a tour of LC's Finno-Ugric collections (D) Article in Journal of Pedantic Librarianship entitled "Government Documents in Lapland: A Statistical Research model" (E) Recording of "New Age Music For Libraries – VOL 2: Atmospheres and Ambient Noise for Loan Hall Environments" (F) MILK & COOKIES,

Device for Conserving energy at Reference desk

Librarian, asked direction to restroom for 20th time in an hour, spots appropriate answer on revolving stock answer indicator (A), and at precise moment, pulls trip wire (B), causing hydraulic glove to goose touchy arboreal hunter (C). Hunter blows dart, pin pointing answer for patron. If patron returns with <u>second</u> question, hunter can be activated again to pin point patron.

Punk librarians Ⓙ groove on gorilla beat and launch into their big hit "Your love is like a *@!!!ƶƶ⚡ serial snag, Baby!"

First that HUCK FINN book, and now this!

Incensed censors fly into moral rage and take matters into their own sweaty hands Ⓚ. Spark from fire lights fuse Ⓛ ⚡

...which ignites L.C.S.H pyrotechnic display Ⓜ. Awed undergrad begins to see the light!

OHHH!

FIZZZZZZ

Ⓜ

But, brilliant as it is, I fully expect to encounter ridicule from my peers! Remember the reaction of my LITA* committee — when I proposed connecting my word processor to my food processor?

It was a very upscale notion at the time, Master!

* Loony Inventors of Technological Apparatus

KQUEEZYNART
SLICE   DICE
EAT

Then there were the infamous 'catalog in a can' experiments...

60% tincture of serial...
50% essence of monograph!
A dash of docs!
A soupçon of manuscripts!
A shake of video!

CREAM OF LIBRARY SOUP

41.

44

Unbound, the creature roamed the countryside, wantonly running up big database searching bills, retro-converting catalogs, and practicing assertiveness training...

Days of bibliographic infamy: A well-meaning library user is discovered alphabetizing the shelf list...

After 10 years of grueling trial and error, Mel Dewey has his breakthrough...

How reference books unwind after hours

Bibliographic singles bar

Mr. Farnsworth pays the price for a life of sloppy serials cataloging.

Saul Popkin goes upscale...

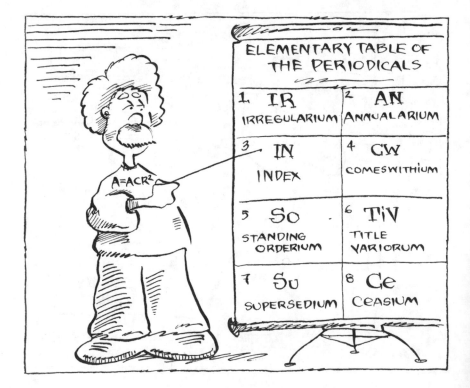

Having never served on an ALA Committee, Horace seriously misunderstood the nature of his first round table appointment.

ACADEMY OF
LIBRARY
ARTS & SCIENCES

BOOKIE
AWARDS

"...And the nominees for the best successive entry cataloging of an irregularly issued Serbo-Croatian government document with separately issued supplements, and semi-annual indexes are..."

Very Special Collections

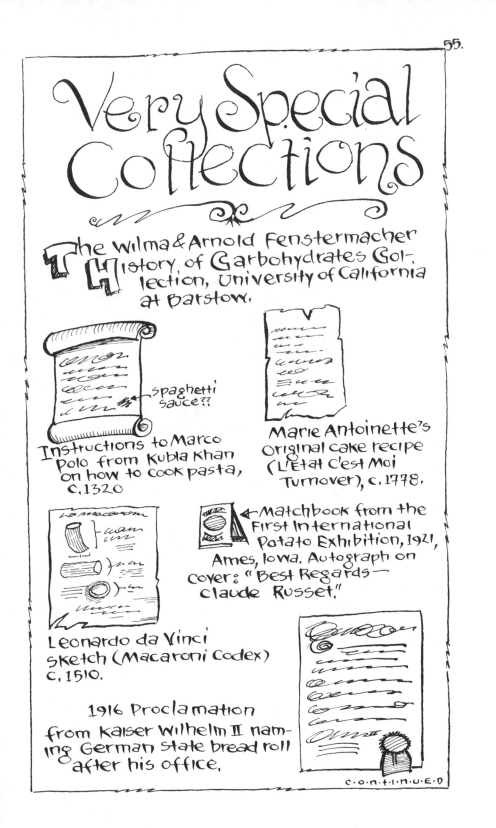

The Wilma & Arnold Fenstermacher History of Carbohydrates Collection, University of California at Barstow.

spaghetti sauce??

Instructions to Marco Polo from Kubla Khan on how to cook pasta, c.1320

Marie Antoinette's Original cake recipe (L'Etat C'est Moi Turnover), c.1778.

Matchbook from the First International Potato Exhibition, 1921, Ames, Iowa. Autograph on cover: "Best Regards— Claude Russet."

Leonardo da Vinci sketch (Macaroni Codex) c.1510.

1916 Proclamation from Kaiser Wilhelm II naming German state bread roll after his office.

c·o·n·t·i·n·u·e·d

56.

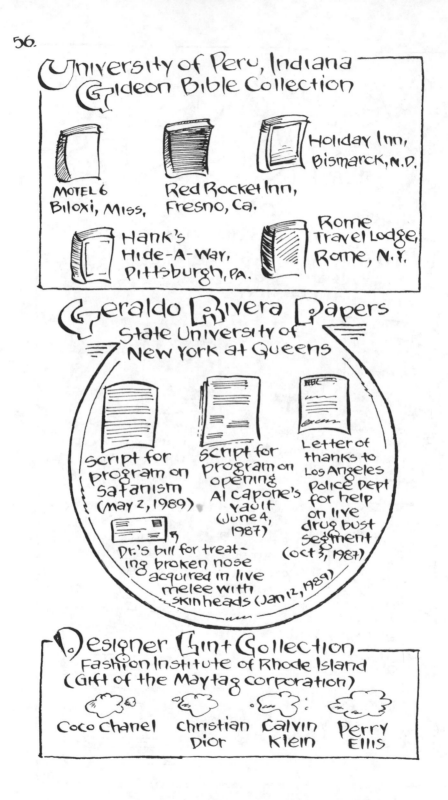

University of Peru, Indiana
Gideon Bible Collection

MOTEL 6
Biloxi, Miss.

Red Rocket Inn,
Fresno, Ca.

Holiday Inn,
Bismarck, N.D.

Hank's
Hide-A-Way,
Pittsburgh, PA.

Rome
Travel Lodge,
Rome, N.Y.

Geraldo Rivera Papers
State University of
New York at Queens

Script for
program on
satanism
(May 2, 1989)

Script for
program on
opening
Al Capone's
vault
(June 4,
1987)

Letter of
thanks to
Los Angeles
Police Dept
for help
on live
drug bust
segment
(Oct 3, 1987)

Dr.'s bill for treat-
ing broken nose
acquired in live
melee with
skinheads (Jan 12, 1989)

Designer Lint Collection
Fashion Institute of Rhode Island
(Gift of the Maytag Corporation)

Coco Chanel

Christian
Dior

Calvin
Klein

Perry
Ellis

57.

One of the seven deadly warning signs of public service burnout.

Games catalogers' kids play: MARC tag

Fred J. Ignatz, eccentric millionaire bibliophile, fulfills a lifelong dream...

62.

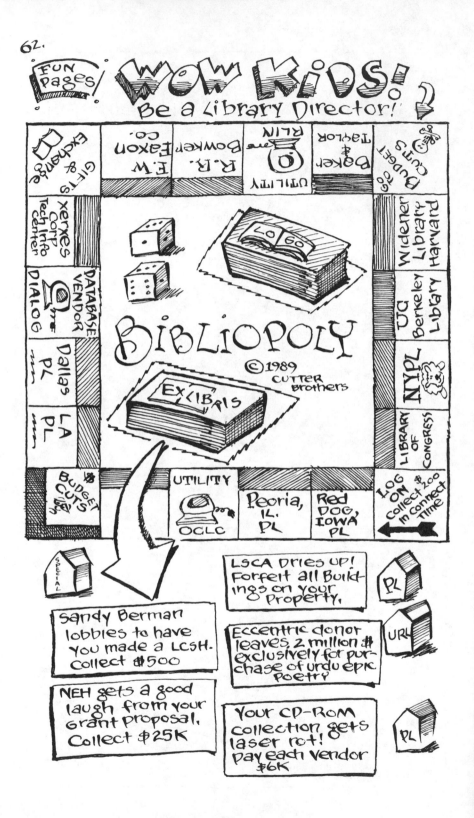

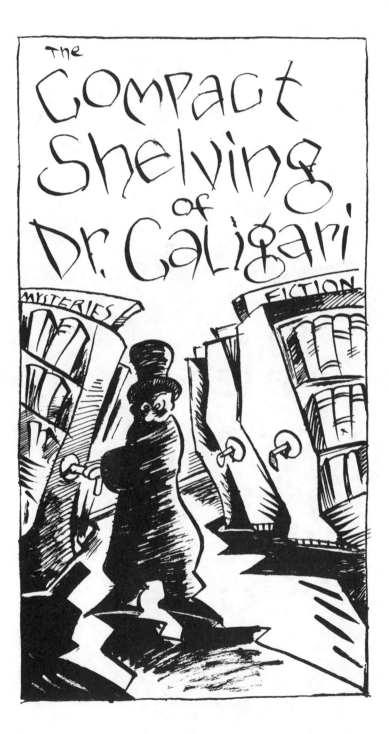

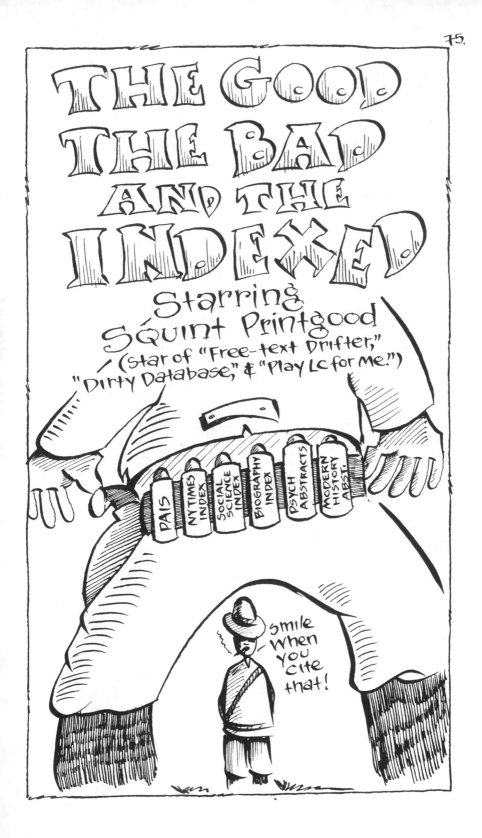

M*E*S*H
ATTENTION!
ATTENTION!
Those wacky medical catalogers of the 4077th will keep you in stitches and headings!
HARVARD
LC
NLM
Johns Hopkins
Hey Hawkeye! Wait'll Hotlips finds what we put between the pages of her thesaurus!
4077
CATALOG DEPT.
BINDERY
U.S.
WELCOME

THE WEREBOOK OF LONDON

Even a tome that
is firmly bound,
and cataloged true
and right
Can transmogrify
when the wolfbane
blooms and
the moon is full
and bright!!

After years of nagging his administration, the librarian of Dingling Brothers Circus is finally put online

The Mid-Pacific Library Network tests CrusoeLine (Computer Reference Utility System Online Environment)

SILICON SITUATIONS

User-hostile interfaces

The Information Explosion

Gone to hardware heaven

Continued

Recommended Reading

1. Barrier, Michael & Martin Williams, eds.
   A Smithsonian Book of Comic-Book Comics.
   New York: Abrams; Smithsonian Institute
   Press, 1981.

2. Berman, Sanford & James Danky, eds. Alterna-
   tive Library Literature: A Biennial Antho-
   logy. Jefferson, N.C.: McFarland & Co., 1982—

3. Canemaker, John. Winsor McCay: His Life &
   Times. New York: Abbeville, 1987

4. Finch, Christopher. The Art of Walt Disney:
   From Mickey Mouse to the Magic Kingdom.
   New York: Abrams, 1973.

5. Lanes, Selma. The Art of Maurice Sendak.
   New York: Abrams, 1980.

6. McDonnell, Patrick, et al. Krazy Kat: The Comic
   Art of George Herriman. New York:
   Abrams, 1986.

7. Rube Goldberg: A Retrospective. New York:
   Putnam, 1983.

8. Rosenberg Harold. Saul Steinberg. New York:
   Knopf, 1978.

9. Rubin, William S. Dada & Surrealist Art. New
   York: Abrams, [1968?].

This book is set in a type style known as <u>Handman Erratic</u>. Named after its developer, Jacob Schmerzgang Handman, infamous "crazed typographer of Lublin," Erratic was first introduced on February 8, 1750, after a night of serious prune brandy imbibing. It is believed that the first font cast was confiscated by the irate local printers guild, and melted down for dental fillings.

The font is characterized by a complete disregard for letter weight consistency, or for standard capital conventions. Also typical are anarchistic baselines, arbitrary serifs, and egregiously wobbly ascenders and descenders.